VERY
BRITISH
PROBLEMS

VERY BRITISH PROBLEMS

MAKING LIFE AWKWARD FOR OURSELVES, ONE RAINY DAY AT A TIME

ROB TEMPLE

Illustrated by Andrew Wightman

sphere

SPHERE

First published in Great Britain in 2013 by Sphere
Reprinted 2013 (four times), 2014 (twice)

Text copyright © Rob Temple, 2013
Illustrations © Andrew Wightman, 2013

The moral right of the author has been asserted.

A CIP catalogue record for this book
is available from the British Library.

ISBN 978-0-7515-5259-1

Typeset in Caslon and Rotis by M Rules
Printed and bound in Great Britain by
Clays Ltd, St Ives plc

Papers used by Sphere are from well-managed forests
and other responsible sources.

MIX
Paper from
responsible sources
FSC® C104740

Sphere
An imprint of
Little, Brown Book Group
Carmelite House
50 Victoria Embankment
London EC4Y 0DZ

An Hachette UK Company
www.hachette.co.uk

www.littlebrown.co.uk

For Rhiain, my family and everyone suffering from Very British Problems.

CONTENTS

INTRODUCTION

Hello, my name is Rob, and I suffer from Very British Problems. If you're reading this, and I'll presume you are, then I'll hazard a guess that you too are suffering from this confusing, distressing and often embarrassing malady.

Before we begin, it's important to know you're far from alone in living with this condition; there are millions of sufferers both in Great Britain and, lest we forget, sometimes further afield.* So do come in, sit down, help yourself to a cup of tea and try to relax. You're safe here.

Let me start by telling you a little about how I first came to study this specific area of neurosis. For years I too thought I was alone in suffering from this strange ailment; debilitated by some sort of severe neurological disorder, some sort of undiagnosed anxiety-related illness – yet no professor, quack, therapist or witch doctor could provide me with a satisfactory diagnosis. So, against all medical advice, I turned to the internet.

You may or may not know that this book, this behavioural study, was born out of a Twitter feed that now goes by the name @soverybritish. Anxious to get to the bottom of things after another long year of awkwardness, I decided, a few days before Christmas 2012, to start posting a few of the strange situations in which my family and I (they are also sufferers, I imagined it was genetic) repeatedly found ourselves.

It was a desperate time. I'm not quite sure what I hoped to achieve. Maybe only that a few people would recognise themselves in the posts and that perhaps we could form a small support group. By the end of January, over 100,000 people were following @soverybritish. As I write, another four months down the line, we've just passed the 300,000 mark. Hundreds of thousands of people, all finding a common bond, all suffering from what I came to refer to as Very British Problems, or as you probably know it by now: VBP.

Bolstered by these extraordinary findings, I

continued to document the common signs of VBP and was soon spotting them everywhere, from the man on the street to historical documents, books, television programmes and films, examples of which are set out in Chapter 19.

When I say you're not alone, I really do mean it.

Many of you may suspect you're only borderline sufferers, and for those in this category there's a test (turn to Chapter 3) which will help you spot the common symptoms and guide you towards a diagnosis. Having said this, I must warn you that tests can prove inconclusive, as people with VBP are often in denial about the severity of their problems.

Regardless of that fact, here's a quick and free consultation to help you decide whether you need this book. If, like me, you: (A) regularly apologise to the person ramming you with their shopping trolley; (B) wake in cold sweats from a nightmare about being invited to 'say a bit about yourself' in a public forum; and (C) are thinking about the weather right at this very instant (don't deny it), then I'm afraid it doesn't look good.

I'm also sorry to have to tell you that there's no cure for VBP. I've often imagined I'm managing the condition, that I have it under control, only to relapse completely without warning. One minute acting like a completely normal human being, the next crippled by nausea at the very idea of finding my reserved seat occupied at the start of a train journey. A train journey I won't even be due to take for another month.

Very British Problems are nigh-on impossible to treat because they're so ingrained in our psyches – tucked away, hidden behind confusing sayings, strange ticks, bizarre customs and double meanings. (If a sufferer of VBP ever tells you they're 'fine', back slowly out of the room.) We're walking, fleshly sacks of volatile madness, just barely held in check, concealed behind stiff upper lips; ready to burst open and bury the streets in a landslide of terrible rage if, heaven forbid, we ever run out of tea.

Why do Very British Problems occur? I'm afraid this book does not deal with the origins of VBP because, quite frankly, I have no idea. I shall leave that conundrum to experts more qualified than I. Indeed, there are many books already available on this very topic. No, this book is simply a guide to self-diagnosis: a way to aid you in spotting a classic case, to help you to get to know your symptoms and to create a picture of what the future may hold. Failing the above, I only hope it provides some comfort.

Good luck. And sorry.

Rob Temple, London, 2013

* Spare a thought for those poor VBP sufferers living abroad, surrounded by relaxed, uninhibited extroverts, going about their daily life with barely a single unnecessary apology passing their lips.

1. PLAYING IT COOL

Calling someone 'fella' or 'pal'
and then unexpectedly having
to enter into a full conversation,
which reveals you're not actually
Cockney at all.

Getting to work early so the least
possible number of people notice you're
wearing a 'trendy' new jacket.

Attempting the 'handshake tip' and dropping your £1 coin on the floor. Best left to Americans . . .

Feeling obliged to ask a taxi driver if they've 'been busy?', but then staying silent for the rest of the journey.

Entering into a mild panic if unable to pick the correct amount of change from your hand within three seconds.

Being told an item is 2-for-1 at the till, leading to you attempting to look elegant while running back through the supermarket searching for a second packet of mince.

Wondering what you've become when a goodbye wave accidentally turns into a bit of a cheeky salute.

Avoiding parks throughout the summer, to reduce the chance of a football rolling over to you.

Panicking and thrusting your hand
up when there's a problem at the
self-service checkout, regardless
of the huge flashing light.

Hoping that you'll look like James Bond every time you put on a dinner jacket, only to end up resembling Ronnie Corbett.

Getting dressed at the speed of light the instant the masseuse says, 'I'll just give you ten minutes to relax.'

Looking into having your hands surgically removed after waving at someone who was waving at someone behind you.

The shame of pulling out of a double-cheek kiss too early, then attempting to re-enter it after the moment's passed.

Calling someone 'geezer' and knowing you haven't pulled it off the instant it leaves your lips.

Nervously hoping not to be seen trying the cash point by the person who just told you it isn't working.

Pretending to be relieved as you agree with the doctor that you don't need the powerful medication you went in specifically to try and obtain.

Feeling it's the right moment to attempt a cheeky wink, regretting it immediately and trying to pretend you actually have something in your eye.

The challenge of attempting to deal with a sneeze while holding a scalding cup of tea in a surface-free area.

Finding yourself doing the twist if left unsupervised on a wedding dance-floor for more than a minute.

Getting a bit too excited when you see your home town on the news.

Deciding to persevere with clasping and shaking the whole appendage when offered a fist-bump by a youngster.

Looking as if you're practising a solo waltz while surreptitiously attempting to remove something unfortunate from your brogue.

Realising you're in the process of exiting a busy lift on the wrong floor and ploughing on regardless.

Running for the bus, missing it and carrying on the run for a short while.

2. RULES OF THE ROAD

Flashing your indicators to thank a fellow motorist, just in case they missed your mini wave, thumbs-up, arm raise and hazard lights.

Taking tremendous pride in your ability to keep your full beam on until the very last possible second.

Looking through the window to the petrol-station forecourt and saying, 'Erm, number . . . four, please,' when you already know exactly what pump you just used.

Arriving at a mini-roundabout at the same time as another driver and knowing you'll be there for some time.

Circling the car park for an hour rather than park half a minute's walk from the entrance.

Unleashing the wave/thumbs-up combo to indicate you're particularly pleased to have been allowed to jog over the zebra crossing.

Feeling genuinely devastated when someone appears to have better knowledge of motorway routes than you.

The dread of flashing a car at night to tell its driver to go first and receiving a flash at exactly the same time, resulting in a flash-off.

Turning to frown and mutter, 'Bloody hell, they were going some,' at any car that drives by slightly faster than the speed limit.

Thanking someone for beeping you when you've failed to notice the lights change.

Feeling the need to indicate despite
being the only car on a deserted B-road.

Getting stuck behind an omni-
speeder who stubbornly drives at
50mph regardless of whether it's a
30mph zone or a 70mph zone.

**Holding your hand up to
your hands-free kit so nobody
thinks you're a lunatic.**

Never, ever being quite sure if it's the right time to use your fog lights.

Feeling guilty for making traffic stop at the lights when you need to cross the road.

The moment you realise you've sat in the front of the wrong sort of taxi, because you didn't want the driver to feel like a chauffeur.

Smashing the hazard button to a pulp every time someone in front of you looks like they may be thinking about braking.

Never once encountering a situation where you have to reverse around a corner since you passed your driving test.

Allowing your car to smash headlong into a truck, rather than relinquish your right of way.

Having an emergency car kit which consists of a tartan blanket, a small box of tissues and a near-empty tin of Victorian travel sweets.

3. THE VERY BRITISH TEST

Are you suffering from severe undiagnosed Britishness? Are you beyond a cure, or are you only presenting the early stages? Take the Very British Test to find out just how bad things are.

(Pick either A, B or C from each of the following and write down how many times you choose each letter. Your most likely malady can be found after the last question.)

1. **Someone bumps into you in the street. Do you:**

   A: Shout, 'Hey Buddy! I'm walking here, fool!'
   B: Think nothing of it; after all, that's just part of the pavement battleground
   C: Raise your palm and apologise while jumping into the road, before going home to shout at the cat and weed the hell out of the garden

2. **You go to make tea and discover that you're out of milk. Do you:**

A: Shrug, go to the cooler and grab a can of Pepsi instead

B: Decide to have an espresso and a couple of biscotti, no big deal

C: Desperately search around the kitchen for a milk alternative, before remembering with great relief that you still have some UHT which you stole from a train

3. **A stranger of the opposite sex gives you a suggestive glance in a bar. Do you:**

A: Smile, wink and ask the bartender to send over a bottle of Bollinger

B: Roll up the sleeves of your shirt and kiss your biceps

C: Try to smile but then back out of the smile midway, then pretend you have a facial twitch to cover up the attempted smile, by which point you've turned remarkably pink

4. **You're unhappy with your meal; it's bland, overcooked and full of unadvertised nuts, which could very well kill you. Do you:**

A: Grab the nearest waiter by the tailcoat and tell him you'll bust his ass unless he gets a rare T-Bone to your table in the next 30 seconds

B: Say you're not fussed; you'll just make do with a carafe of Pinot Noir and a Gauloises

C: Complain quietly to your dining companion, tell the waiter the food is perfect and feel quietly thankful you brought your EpiPen

5. **It's a bank holiday weekend and you have Monday off work. Do you plan to:**

A: Load up the pick-up, drive into the countryside, fish, swim in the lake and tell horror stories around a roaring fire

B: Lie in bed all weekend, having sex (sans socks), writing poetry and eating pain au chocolat by the dozen

C: Paint the spare room before drinking studiously at the local boozer, safe in the knowledge that Tuesday will never, ever come

6. **Someone has just pushed in front of you in a long queue. What's your reaction?**

A: What's a queue?
B: What's a queue?
C: Feeling like you're about to faint with the silent rage pulsing through you, only noticeable by the throbbing vein on your forehead

7. **You're in a training session and are encouraged to say a bit about yourself. Do you:**

A: Start with how your grandparents met and go from there, ending with a monologue about how you still aren't in the right place to really know your emotional self

B: Say nothing. Because you're not even in the training session. Because you like to sleep late on Tuesdays

C: Say your name and your job title, then close your eyes until someone else starts speaking

8. **You're not feeling your best and decide to visit your doctor. What's the outcome?**

A: You leave with a prescription for Prozac, Xanax, Vicodin, Ritilin and ten sessions with an eminent psychiatrist

B: You're told that despite a lifelong diet consisting of meat, cheese and brandy, you seem to be in top condition for a 92-year-old

C: You tell him/her you're absolutely fine and there's no need for alarm, then leave and collapse in reception due to blood loss

9. You've been told you haven't long to live. What do you do?

A: Plan to get your memoir finished as soon as possible, before visiting every member of your extended family and completing all 352 items on your bucket list

B: Nothing, you didn't plan to live beyond 30 anyhow

C: Quietly say 'bugger', compare your lifespan to a cricket score and then decide to start drinking full-fat milk, before thinking better of it

10. Someone is sitting in your reserved train seat. Do you:

A: Pick them up and shove them into the luggage rack, before finishing off their half-eaten sandwich

B: Sit next to them, get on like a house on fire and end up telling the story on your wedding day

C: Hover in the vestibule outside the toilet hoping another seat will become available somewhere between London and Edinburgh

11. You're in a new sandwich shop and there's an impatient queue forming. Do you:

A: Order your usual: a Philly cheese steak foot-long on brown, ranch dressing, hold the onions, over easy, toasted, Diet Coke, no ice, to go, and ask them to make it snappy

B: Ask for the special of the day, or whatever they recommend

C: Panic and end up with a sweetcorn,

Marmite and pickled egg bap, for which you manage to pay £11. Then go to M&S

12. **Someone is holding a door for you from quite a distance. What's your response?**

A: Walk slowly and casually to the door and slip a few dollar bills in the stranger's top pocket as you pass through
B: Walk slowly and casually through the door, without making eye contact
C: Sprint to the door, laugh slightly, apologise and then say 'after you'

13. **Which of these most closely resembles your behaviour on the London Underground transport system?**

A: Shouting, 'Hey, does anyone know how to get to Ly-ses-ter Square?!' across the carriage while rearranging your bum-bag
B: Gesticulating wildly at the gentleman who just stepped on your flip-flops
C: Silently staring at the map on the carriage wall to make sure there's absolutely no chance of making eye contact with anyone

14. Which of these most resembles the contents of your kitchen cupboards?

A: Squirty cheese, cans of bread, a 1 kilogram bag of Doritos, Pop Tarts and a crate of Mountain Dew

B: Empty. There's half a ciabatta out on a wooden chopping board, but you eat everything else as soon as you buy it

C: Three hundred and twenty four bags for life and a near-empty bottle of HP sauce

15. A fellow motorist lets you pull out in front of them. What's your response?

A: I wouldn't notice them from so high up in my truck

B: I wouldn't notice them because I haven't looked in my mirrors for about seven years

C: Thank them with every flashy device my car has, as if they've just donated me a kidney

How did you answer?

Mostly A You're confident, aggressive, you know what you want and you don't take guff from anyone. In fact, you're so far from British you're positively American, and sure to enjoy a fulfilled life devoid of awkwardness.

Mostly B There's some suggestion that you might present the early signs of Britishness, but you're still way off a full-blown attack. With your *laissez faire* attitude and raw sensuality, you're not afraid to take a risk and to hell with the consequences. You'd almost certainly be happier residing in somewhere like France or Italy.

Mostly C We're afraid it's bad news: you're show-
ing many symptoms of Very British
Problems and you're doomed to a life of
apology and repression. There's no cure,
and it doesn't wear off with time; terribly sorry about that, old bean.

4. BOOZE BRITAIN

Sneaking a few empties into your regular bin bag so the recycling collectors won't think you have a drinking problem.

Wondering if it's acceptable for you to have a glass of wine with breakfast because they do it on *Saturday Kitchen*.

Not fancying a whole bottle of wine so just buying three mini bottles instead.

Strictly not drinking in January. Except for beer and wine. And gin for a treat . . .

Saying you'd build a pub in your house every time someone asks you what you'd do if you won the lottery.

Telling the nearest tourist, at any given opportunity, that Brits used to drink beer because the water was unclean.

Feeling too embarrassed to ask for just alcohol from the train's refreshment trolley, so also buying the entire range of sandwiches and throwing them away later.

The shameful feeling when you have to make two trips to the payment area at the off-licence.

Having a Bucks Fizz on Christmas morning and thinking it wouldn't hurt to start every day in similar fashion.

Saying you'll 'just' have a gin and tonic, as if you're part of a temperance movement.

Protesting that the only reason you've started making Pimm's in a pint glass is because there's more room for fruit.

Not drinking on a Friday night and feeling jealous of people looking rough on Saturday morning.

Convincing everyone that Trivial Pursuit is a good idea, simply because it guarantees you'll still be in the pub for at least another seven hours.

Waking with a hangover so ferocious you briefly consider giving up drinking until teatime.

An unshakable conviction that one can drink away a cold.

Saying you're going for a 'cheeky pint', meaning you won't be home until Tuesday.

Owning a glass for every type of drink ever concocted.

Saying you only ever eat bacon when you're hungover, then working out you're getting through fifteen pigs a month.

Moving at cheetah speed
to save the half-inch of flat
beer from being swiped by
the barmaid, then feeling
ashamed.

Thinking gin and tonic in a can
is the most acceptable mode of
daytime drinking, because people
might mistake it for an energy
drink.

5. OFFICE ETIQUETTE

Switching from 'kind regards' to 'regards' as a warning that you're dangerously close to losing your temper.

Being allowed to expense things at work, but not doing it because you don't want to be a bother.

Taking your food out of the office microwave while it's still quite cold, so as not to keep the queue waiting.

Sending someone an angry email, seeing them before they've read it . . . Pretending everything's fine.

Calculating the correct amount of time to stand up so as not to appear callous when someone brings a baby into the office.

Waiting for everybody to go out at lunch so nobody has to witness you eating at your desk like a starving hippo.

Wishing you were able to resist quipping, 'Morning!' when someone has left the office but has had to immediately return to collect a forgotten item.

Writing a terribly modest CV, for fear of appearing boastful.

Being unable to eat crisps at your desk without worrying that your mouth sounds like a building site.

Being asked which floor you need in a lift, saying 'three, please,' while pressing the button yourself.

Feeling compelled to actually say the word 'delete' when deleting something.

Saying that you 'didn't get up to much' over the weekend, despite achieving more than you ever have in a two-day period.

The phrase: 'We're going to put you into groups with people you don't normally get a chance to work with.'

Only ever filling your bottle up to halfway at the water cooler because you can't stand the pressure.

Walking back into the office after having a slightly shorter haircut than normal.

Feeling compelled
to do an exaggerated
tip-toe mime out
of a meeting room
when you've received
a phone call you have
to take.

Automatically finding your work pals and larking around like excited school children in the playground when forced outside for a fire drill.

Noticing your boss about to take the lift so taking the stairs, despite being on the 37th floor.

Carrying your £400 iPad to work and back every single day, but never once removing it from your bag for fear of looking ostentatious.

Giving a trainer five stars across the board on the evaluation form, despite them falling asleep for a good portion of the afternoon and smelling strongly of port.

Returning to your desk to find
someone sitting in your chair
while talking to the person you sit
next to . . . deciding to go away
for a bit longer.

Deciding to show your colleagues the
real you, so switching to a particularly
jazzy desktop background.

Handing in your notice after suspecting someone has used your mug.

6. BRITISH RAIL DISASTERS

Glowering at the Quiet Coach
sign in the hope it will cause
a chatterbox to be ejected
through the roof of the train.

Standing ready to exit the train a full ten minutes before your station.

Waiting for the person reading the paper over your shoulder to finish before turning the page.

The paralysing fear of discovering your train has been replaced by a bus.

Simply closing your eyes on the tube to shield yourself from the possibility of looking at someone.

Sitting in someone's reserved seat and feeling sheer terror until the train has been moving for at least ten minutes.

The 'stay put or move' conundrum when the train empties, leaving you sitting unnecessarily with a stranger.

Resigning yourself to an unusual and arduous train route, rather than risk sharing your commute home with a colleague.

Sitting awkwardly for your entire journey to accommodate the staggering leg spread of the gentleman beside you.

Repeatedly pressing the door button on the train before it's illuminated, to assure your fellow commuters you have the situation in hand.

Requesting, when prompted, a forward-facing window seat while knowing in your heart it will have no bearing whatsoever on the seat you'll be assigned.

Feeling immensely proud to be able to show the ticket inspector that you've paid your way.

The struggle to comprehend why Quiet Coach rules are abandoned when the train becomes crowded.

Knowing that no matter what time of day it is or which carriage you pick, there will always be someone next to you eating chips.

Jerking quickly away from the door and looking at the wall when someone exits the lavatory, in an attempt to convince them you haven't been waiting and just enjoy relaxing in that part of the train.

Drinking at the counter in the buffet carriage as if it's an actual bar.

Only persevering with rail travel due to bus timetables resembling one of the harder codes assigned to Russell Crowe in *A Beautiful Mind.*

Discovering your reserved seat on the train has been occupied by someone who looks quite settled, so you stand.

The mass relief when someone is brave enough to open the train window when the carriage is hotter than a pizza oven.

Getting stuck on a train for three days because a swan in the next county has decided to sit quite near the track.

Feeling like you've just won the FA Cup when you haven't got a ticket and the barriers are open.

The disappointment of finding the train company has reserved you a seat next to another human.

The alarming moment someone talks to you on the tube.

Subtly glancing at the luggage rack to indicate to the person next to you that you're going to have to get up soon.

Feeling compelled to purchase the entire snack section of M&S before embarking on any train journey longer than 15 minutes.

7. VERY HISTORICAL BRITISH PROBLEMS

Making Life Awkward for Ourselves, One Rainy Day at a Time (Since Records Began)

2012

During the Olympics, Londoners have to deal with the terrifying daily threat of Americans talking out loud on the capital's public transport systems, coupled with the shock of unprecedented sporting success.

The Queen's Diamond Jubilee takes place during the British summertime. To celebrate, Her Majesty stands on a barge and sails very slowly down the Thames. A fly-past is due to take place but is cancelled due to the apocalyptic sky and lashing rain.

2009

The *Telegraph* begins publishing MPs' expenses. While most Brits feel it's too bothersome to claim for small items at work, politicians are found to have claimed for an ice-cube tray (£1.50), a packet of ginger biscuits (67p) and a small bag of horse manure (70p), as well as many rather more extravagant items, such as moat cleaning (£2,115) and maintenance on a lawnmower (£598).

2007

The smoking ban arrives, meaning Brits need never express their displeasure at others smoking through the medium of coughing, tutting and glowering again.

2001

The England football team beat Germany five goals to one, in Germany, and so begins a decade of English dominance in world football. Oh . . .

2000

7 August: the day it rained fish in Great Yarmouth. Retired ambulance driver Fred Hodgkins, who had his garden covered in silver sprats, describes the scenes as 'quite extraordinary'.

1992

The first ever text message is sent, meaning from this year forth Brits are able to express something nearing emotion without the horror of having to look anyone in the face.

1988

The pound note is withdrawn from circulation, resulting in widespread panic as Brits now have even more coins to count at the till within the three-second limit before 'critical-level flustering' occurs.

1986

The M25 – the most moaned-about motorway in British history – opens. Brits immediately start blaming it for why they've been turning up for work two hours late every day.

1971

The United Kingdom decimalises its currency. In a bid to help people with the change from what we refer to today as 'old money', a publicity campaign kicks into full swing weeks before Decimalisation Day, which includes the catchily titled Max Bygraves song, 'Decimalisation'.

1969

The Beatles perform for the last time as a four-piece on the rooftop of their Savile Row headquarters. Police make their way to the building and try to bring the final concert from the biggest band ever to a close, because it is disrupting local businesses' lunch hours.

1966

England win the World Cup. People across the country celebrate by taking to the streets and eating sandwiches with their neighbours.

1950

The first mass package holidays abroad begin during the 1950s. By 1970 Brit have invaded Spain, Portugal and Greece. Echoes of chips being demanded with fry-ups and laughter at differently named breakfast cereals can be heard ricocheting across western Europe.

1939–1945

During the Second World War, brave Brits demonstrate what comes to be known as Dunkirk or Blitz Spirit, terms still used today to describe those who stoically soldier into work through literally millimetres of snow.

1930

The first *Times* crossword gives people something to concentrate on when travelling on public transport, to prevent anyone accidentally talking to one another.

1895

The first car ride in Britain prompts the inaugural thumbs-up/mini wave combo as a way of saying 'thank you ever so for letting me have my right of way'. The first speeding fine comes one year later, delivered to a Mr Arnold from East Peckham, caught travelling at a lunatic speed of eight miles an hour. He is chased down over five miles by a constable on his bicycle.

1871

The first ever bank holiday. Brits celebrate by doing some shoddy DIY and then filling themselves with gin.

1863

The London Underground opens between Paddington and Farringdon, using gas-lit wooden carriages hauled by steam locomotives. It carries 38,000 passengers on the opening day, with not a single one of their 76,000 eyes making contact.

1878

The first weekly weather forecast in the UK. It tells of the rainiest week since records began.

1843

The printing of the first edition of the *News of the World*. The first telephone call, *ahem*, is made 33 years later.

1840

Postal service begins in Britain, bringing with it the first complaint about the cost of stamps. Even now, Brits consider 60 pence to take a letter from one side of the county to the other, in one day, to be wholly unreasonable.

1822

First edition of *The Sunday Times*. Brits who buy it immediately sort 99 per cent of it into the bin, before turning to the page where Winner's Dinners will eventually end up and patiently waiting 171 years for its arrival.

1814

The London Beer Flood sees 1.46 million litres of beer burst from vats and flood central London, originating from Tottenham Court Road. Despite at least seven people drowning, most Brits would still choose this (ideally coupled with an explosion at a nearby Dry Roasted Peanut factory) as the way they'd like to go.

1797

Nelson is shot in the right arm by a musket ball during the Battle of Santa Cruz de Tenerife. He is rowed to a surgeon's ship and while being helped aboard declares, 'Let me alone! I have got my legs left and one arm.' Most of his right arm is then amputated and within half an hour he's back issuing orders to his captains. He'd lost his eye three years previously.

1755

Samuel Johnson's dictionary is published. Ten-year-olds across the country immediately flock to snigger at the words 'sex', 'bum' and 'willy'.

1707

The first parliament of Great Britain sees MPs begin claiming expenses for everything from a new hat (two shillings) to horse maintenance (one guinea). (*See also*: 2009.)

1665

The Great Plague rampages through London, causing thousands to complain of feeling 'a bit peaky' while saying 'I'll survive', before keeling over and dying rather horribly.

1660

The first ever documented tea break, courtesy of Samuel Pepys, who notes that after a gruelling session at the office he 'did send for a cup of tee [sic] (a China drink) of which I never had drank before'. Whether or not he dunked a biscuit remains a matter of debate.

1609

Shakespeare's sonnets are published. Brits struggle to deal with proclamations as saucy and forthright as suggesting the person they fancy is more lovely and temperate than a summer's day, regardless of the fact that the best summer's day in 1609 is a slightly cloudy 14°C, turning a bit chillier in the evening.

1604

Word's first railway inaugurated, running two miles from Strelley to Wollaton in Nottinghamshire. It arrives half an hour late, single noblemen take up a whole tables of four to themselves and buffet-cart sandwiches, even though not yet invented, cost a whopping half crown and four groats.

1586

Tobacco hits English society, prompting people to begin practising their apologies for not having a lighter.

1066–1563

Mostly just a lot of battles (about 55 of them) and Henry VIII marries six women (a few of them he doesn't get on at all well with).

1066

The Dark Ages come to an end as William the Conqueror defeats King Harold II at the Battle of Hastings, the earliest date every Brit has forged into his/her consciousness because it's an easy number to remember.

8. UNWRITTEN RULES (AND WHEN THEY'RE BROKEN)

The unwelcome surprise of someone telling you how they are after you've asked them how they are.

Revealing you don't like tea and being stared at as if you've just pissed on the table.

Not being able to help saying 'oops!' when someone else drops something.

Saying 'cheers' to whoever's in the lift as the doors open at your floor.

Pausing your conversation for the duration of a journey in a crowded lift.

The confusing moment when, on a whim, you decide to experiment with a double-handed handshake, followed by an upper-arm grab.

Being required by law to drink ferociously on the last day of a bank holiday, even though you have work the next day.

No longer smiling when the camera hasn't worked for a third time, yet still forcing out the word 'cheese'.

Feeling very uneasy while honouring a request for three sugars.

Wondering why washing-machine minutes last roughly quarter of an hour.

Not quite catching someone's name, meaning you can never speak to them again.

The anxious bewilderment when clocking a stranger deciding to queue at your side rather than behind you.

Feeling the need to pat down all your pockets, despite knowing full well you haven't got your loyalty card.

Knowing it's time to leave the party when someone gets out their guitar.

The pressure of trying to get your seatbelt on, adjust the mirror and drive away from a visit to your family, while all of your relatives stand in the doorway waving.

Having to say the word 'bye' at least three times when hanging up the telephone, getting quieter with each one.

Never under any circumstances looking at people in the vehicles to your left or right when eating in a fast-food establishment's car park.

Informing someone their flies
are undone by using subtle eye
movements, codewords and a
variety of coughs.

Getting out your tool box and causing
hundreds of pounds worth of damage
to your house because it's bank holiday
Monday.

Having at least one friend who
always insists on either go-karting
or paintball for his birthday.

Calling someone 'mate' forever because you're worried you might pronounce their name incorrectly.

The curious situation when someone is still holding on to your hand despite the handshake being long over.

Proclaiming, 'Oh wow, excellent!' whenever someone responds to your question about where they're from, then having to say 'no' when they ask if you've been.

People you don't know who
think it appropriate to mix
a hug into a handshake.

9. PAVEMENT PITFALLS

Tripping up over nothing and turning to stare furiously at the floor.

Seeing someone you know walking just ahead you, so stopping dead in the street until they're completely out of sight.

Wishing someone goodbye and
then leaving in the same direction.

Spending your life squeezing
past people, yet never once
completing the sentence:
'Excuse me, sorry, do you
mind if I just . . . ?'

Being unable to turn and walk in the
opposite direction without first taking
out your phone and frowning at it.

Reluctantly slowing your walk
slightly when sensing a fast-paced
stranger about to overtake.

Coming face to face with a fellow pedestrian and breaking into an impromptu 'oops, we've moved to the same side' street dance.

Walking a mile in the wrong direction because there hasn't been an appropriate time to interrupt your friend to say goodbye.

Trying not to frown at toddlers in our nation's capital, as they repeatedly run over your feet with their tiny scooters.

Coughing when walking down a pavement at night to indicate to the person ahead of you that you're there and you're definitely not going to attack them. Result: they immediately think you're going to attack them.

Apologising profusely for slamming into the back of a gentleman who has decided he must stop dead in his tracks.

Thinking that giving a stranger *some* directions is better than none, despite having no idea where you've just sent them.

Chuckling heartily after walking into
a lamp post, despite a strong suspicion
you've broken your cheek.

**Turning to find the person
you've been talking to for
the last couple of minutes
stopped to look in a shop
about 20 metres ago.**

The fear of suspecting you may have just
placed some rubbish in the wrong type
of bin.

Jumping into the path of a car
rather than walking in front of
someone taking a photograph.

Finding yourself walking at the same pace
as a stranger so immediately hurling yourself
through the nearest shop window.

Expertly turning a trip into a gentle jog.

Needing to back turn in the direction you've just come so using a shop as a makeshift roundabout.

Dropping five pence: Pick it up and look desperate, or leave it and look like a snob?

Seeing a friend further down the pavement and ignoring them until they're near, to avoid having to do a wave/laugh/mini-jog for any longer than necessary.

Lobbying your MP for a special lane to accommodate people pulling wheelie-bags.

The moment of split-second panic wondering if the automatic door is going to open or not.

Knowing you've just received wholly incorrect directions and heading off that way anyway so as not to cause offence.

10. PUBLIC HOUSE HAZARDS

Being in the same round as someone who finds it hard swallowing lots of liquid, yet insists on drinking pints.

Feeling utterly devastated when you say to the barman, 'I think this guy was next,' and you're not thanked.

Being required by law to have a pint and a fry-up in an airport, regardless of the fact that it's 6 a.m. and you fancy neither.

Going in to a pub to use the loo
and pretending to look for a
friend all the way into the toilet.

Not being able to eat pork scratchings
without someone telling you they're
disgusting.

Opting to try something other
than your usual and immediately
realising you've just ruined your
only bond with the bar staff.

Asking to sample an ale, disliking it and ordering a whole pint so as not to further waste the barman's time.

Being alarmingly over-enthusiastic when able to tell the stranger that, 'Yes, this seat is free, and you may take it.'

Thanking someone on being told that, 'Yes, this seat is free, and you may take it,' as if they've just given you a kidney.

Being accused of alcoholism because you've ordered a soft drink.

The crushing disappointment of saying, 'Oh, whatever you're having,' and ending up with a coffee.

Only ever carrying two empty glasses back to the bar using the index and middle fingers of one hand, to show you're a professional.

The fear of placing 50 pence on the edge of the pool table and the stranger playing saying, 'You can play the winner.'

Being told a higher price for a second
round of drinks identical to the first,
asking, 'Are you sure?' and paying it
anyway.

Ordering food despite having
just eaten, purely because your
companion asked, 'Is anyone else
eating?' and you don't want to
leave a man behind.

The embarrassment of the barman
disappearing out back to answer your
query regarding the establishment's crisp
flavours, when you already know full
well you're ordering ready salted.

Thinking that using a tray in a pub is a sign of weakness.

Calling a square foot of concrete a 'beer garden'.

Ordering yourself a whole bottle when told there's a £10 card limit. Pretending you didn't know about it.

Vowing to hunt down the pub's board-game dice thief and give him a damn good thrashing.

Wiping your hands on your trousers to assure everyone you've washed, despite the hand dryer for once rendering them completely dry.

Expressing your surprise at your £5-pint by loudly saying 'FIVE POUNDS?!' while handing over £5.

Having to open your bag of crisps to the whole table, regardless of personal hunger, providing a ration of two per person.

11. VERY BRITISH WEATHER

The 10 Types of Highly Problematic Meteorological Phenomena Every Brit Must Suffer

Name: Ghost Rain

Description: As this type of rain is invisible to the naked eye, you won't be prepared for it. You will only know Ghost Rain is occurring when you get half a mile from your house and realise your newspaper has shed its ink, your top has become transparent and you're scrunching up your face like a Shar Pei in a wind tunnel.

Most likely: March/April.

Name: Rehearsal Sun (aka Derren Brown Sun)

Description: Before you even wake you'll sense the UV bashing against your windows. Throwing open the curtains, warm light will flood your bedroom. As dust dances in the sun's bountiful beams, you throw on a linen shirt and your best straw hat and bounce outside, whereby you're smacked with an icy blast so strong you think you've been sucked from a plane.

Most likely: March/October.

Name: Dark Horse Sun

Description: 'At last!' you'll exclaim, a day both mildly warm *and* bright, the first of the year in fact. Your colleagues suggest a lunchtime beverage in the Windsor Castle, because it has that little outdoor area. After a quick shandy and a few laughs in the warm sun you head back to the office, whereupon your secretary informs you that, of course, your face is now the colour of a London bus.
Most likely: May/June.

Name: Insane Rain

Description: This violent, loud, show-off rain does not care who you are. It will appear suddenly, without warning, even when it was sunny just minutes ago. It has no morals or emotion. If you're caught in it you'll instinctively start running, even if there's nowhere to go. If you're inside, everyone in the room will move slowly towards the window and stare out with their hands on hips. Some people may even take photographs. It'll be the first thing you talk about with anyone you meet for weeks to come.
Most likely: About twice a year, anytime between March and November.

Name: 'Bloody Hell It's Cold' Cold

Description: This name of this type of cold is shouted on average three times per day while it occurs: once on the way to work, once on the way to lunch, and once on leaving work. You'll know it's happening because you'll turn slightly sideways as you walk into its arctic gusts, like some hideous, gloved, purple-faced crab who longs to be placed in a pot of boiling water.

Most likely: 80 per cent of the year.

Name: Lost Sun

Description: This sun is so named because it's meant to be in Melbourne but has accidentally taken a wrong turn and ended up in Britain for a day, causing its inhabitants to mope around like dying bumblebees while tarmac bubbles on the road. Sleeping will be impossible and at any given second someone, somewhere, will be comparing the heat to the summer of 1976.

Most likely: A single day in July.

Name: Mystery Ice

Description: Mystery Ice strikes when you least expect it. You'll be walking along quite merrily and then suddenly your legs will be above your head and a rude word will be hurling itself from your mouth. You'll lie in a star shape and laugh to let others know you're perfectly fine with the situation, despite a suspicion you've just destroyed your coccyx.
Most likely: November to March.

Name: One Shade of Grey

Description: You'll recognise this phenomenon through an inability to tell where the pavement ends and the sky begins. Nothing has ever been achieved on a One Shade of Grey day, so if you notice one upon opening your curtains the best advice is to climb back into bed, drink gin through a straw and remember the 'Lost Sun' days of years past.
Most likely: Any of the 18 months of winter.

Name: Narnia Snow

Description: The most talked about of all the weather conditions in British media; the anticipation that builds towards this phenomenon is gargantuan.

When it falls, burying everything in literally milli-metres of snow, trains cease to run, all the salt we forgot to store runs out and everyone pretends they can't get to work, while news coverage consists of a looped interview with a man in Cumbria who had to dig his car out of the drive and a cold reporter stand-ing next to a pile of grit.

Most likely: February

Name: London Snow

Description: While the countryside wakes up to layers of pure white alpine loveliness, cities have to make do with a dandruffy scattering which quickly turns into grey slush, causing urban children to softly weep as they construct charcoal-coloured snowmen matted with smog, cigarette butts and guilt, result-ing in row upon row of sludgy Albert Steptoes.

Most likely: February

12. WAITER WOES

Waking up in cold sweats remembering the time your dining companion sent some food back to the kitchen.

Pointing at your choice on the menu instead of saying what you'd like, so as not to appear extravagant.

Losing the power of speech while waiting for a waiter's card machine to work.

Leaving it at least a week before publicly stating that, on reflection, your main course wasn't quite up to scratch.

The compulsion to be ridiculously friendly to a waiter who has just been treated rudely by a neighbouring table.

Ordering one of the specials so the waitress won't have wasted her time reciting them.

Summarising that you, 'Wouldn't say it tasted great,' to indicate it's possibly the most revolting dish you've ever encountered.

Attempting to telepathically communicate your embarrassment to the waiter when he asks your table if you're ready to order and everyone keeps chatting.

The small
embarrassed smile
reserved for fellow
diners who have
noticed your failed
attempt to catch a
waiter's attention.

Asking for the bill by moving your lips and miming with your hands, because using actual sound would be vulgar.

Feeling you must blow your cheeks out, pat your stomach, laugh and tell the waiter you're stuffed, rather than just say you don't wish to have a pudding on this occasion.

Saying yes to a side portion of chips, despite your main course being almost completely made up of potato.

The panic of knowing exactly what you're going to order because you've been looking at the website for a whole week, then finding you've been looking at an old menu.

Trying to feel happy about bagging a reservation in the hottest restaurant in town, despite your table being in the toilet.

Not being able to cope when there are two of you in a tapas bar and you're given three of everything.

Taking an extraordinary length of time putting your coat while you wait for a good moment to shout 'thanks' towards the till area.

The annoying moment a dining companion insists the meal will be on them, meaning you'll no longer be choosing the expensive thing you want.

Receiving a main course which is not at all like you envisioned and fighting not to look like you've just been told your dog has died.

Debating whether or not to tell the waiter that your wine tastes a bit like bleach, then remembering you only paid £60 for it.

The exhausting, 'Honestly, I don't mind where I sit,' stand-off before commencing your meal.

13. SHOPPING SLIP-UPS

Saying hello to a friend in the supermarket, then creeping around like a burglar to avoid seeing them again.

Thanking someone for letting you go
first when you were already ahead of
them in the queue.

Hoping you didn't come across
as too monstrous when you told
the shop assistant you were just
browsing.

Trying not to be rude when
you have 28 items in your
basket, no bag and are asked
if you need a bag.

Not correcting someone when they mistake you for a shop assistant.

Thanking the cash point for bestowing your money.

Accidentally ripping off two tickets at the delicatessen counter and making the split second decision to leave town immediately.

Not being able to fit food in half your kitchen cupboards because they're being used to store 83 bags for life.

Finding someone examining the goods you need in the supermarket, so pretending to inspect another item until they leave.

Worrying you'll be suspected a thief if exiting a shop without making a purchase.

Being incapable of placing your items on the counter in a newsagent's without saying, 'Just these, please.'

Deciding against a bag of crisps as you have nothing smaller than a tenner and don't want to cause any bother.

Only ever saying 'thanks' and 'you're welcome' at whispering volume during the placement of the Next Customer Please divider.

Apprehensively approaching someone to ask if they're in the queue as if creeping towards a firework that hasn't gone off.

Feeling guilty using a bag for life that doesn't match the supermarket you're in.

Loudly tapping your fingers at the cash point, to assure the queue that you've asked for money and the wait is out of your hands.

Not taking the last of anything in the supermarket, in case someone else needs it.

Feeling embarrassed to have nicer food than the person behind you at the checkout.

The childish urge to start entering your pin number before being prompted by the cashier.

Feeling obliged to put a product in your basket after trying a free sample, then depositing it on a random shelf and hoping you're not arrested.

Patiently queuing in a queue that turns out not to be a queue at all.

Apologising to the cashier for not having your own bag as if you've been having an affair with his wife.

Realising you've entered the wrong establishment and having to pretend to look around for a bit.

Considering handing yourself in despite the shop alarm having nothing to do with you.

Being very dramatic about taking your phone in and out your jacket so it doesn't look like you're pocketing chocolate bars.

Standing back as if you've just activated an old World War II bomb as the assistant goes to verify your age at the self-service checkout.

14. KEEPING CALM AND CARRYING ON

Failing to understand someone, begging their pardon three times and then just nodding and smiling.

Falling over and apologising to the person helping you up.

Going to your doctor and
replying, 'I'm fine, thank you,'
when they ask how you are.

**Pressing the bus bell a stop
too early; alighting and
continuing your journey on
foot.**

Lying in a star shape for a bit and
laughing after slipping over, to let
everyone know you're absolutely fine
with what's just happened.

Translating 'carpe diem' as 'treat yourself to a slightly more expensive load of bread'.

Saying you're pleased with your haircut despite the deep inner sadness it's causing you.

Telling your doctor you're feeling a bit better, so as not to question their treatment plan.

Not quibbling with the unexpectedly high price, despite being certain your choices fully adhere to the rules of the Meal Deal.

Feeling you need a change in your life, so treating yourself to a completely new type of cheese.

Saying 'left' and 'right' at random, rather than admit to the optician that all the lenses seem identical.

Assuring your hairdresser that the water temperature is fine, despite a strong suspicion that your scalp is beginning to melt.

Locking yourself in the wardrobe until you're certain that the window cleaner has finished and left.

Feeling genuinely terrified that one day Sir David Attenborough won't be on television anymore, but trying not to think about it.

Saying, 'It's nothing, really . . . ' to indicate you're seconds from losing consciousness.

The desperate moment, on realising you're out of milk, when you scan the kitchen wondering: 'Is there *anything* here that can be made into milk?'

Inexplicably lying about seeing the match last night and praying you don't encounter any detailed questions about it during the ensuing conversation.

Worrying how we'll end any major celebration when Paul McCartney isn't around to sing 'Hey Jude'.

Feeling awful at your desk and hoping you'll be told to go home, yet replying, 'I'll survive,' when asked how you're feeling.

Not batting an eyelid as you silently eat every last one of the chips everyone saw you accidentally pour sugar on.

The moment everyone hears that you've just accidentally ripped your newspaper in half during an especially vigorous page turn.

15. TEN VERY BRITISH THINGS WE PRETEND TO ENJOY ...

... But Love to Moan About

1: The sun

When the old boy finally pops out for one day in May, warming us to the dizzy heights of 17°C, Brits are sent into frenzy. Roofs are sawn off cars and gloves thrown to the sea as we rejoice at the death of 18 months of winter. A dash to the supermarket reveals a bare shelf where the Pimm's used to be, surrounded by distraught Brits (and always one gentleman not wearing a top) wondering if brandy will do more or less the same trick. Venture to the meat aisle and all you'll find is a single sausage, spinning like the number plate at the end of *Back to the Future*. By the third mild day we're already complaining it's 'just a bit too hot', we've been told we've caught the sun (translation: have burned to a crisp) and are once again pining over big coats, pub fires and frost. Repeat *ad infinitum*.

2: Mini-breaks

You finish work on a Friday evening and jump in the motor, zooming straight into heavy traffic for five hours. When you finally get to the Cotswolds, your relationship on the brink, you can't find the B&B so spend the night in the car. On waking you find you're parked outside the B&B, which seems to have found the photograph on its website by typing 'nice B&B' into Google Images. After walking eight miles along a grass verge you reach the Dog & Duck. Placing your straw boater on the bar you ask the landlord for a pint of the Old Mad Hen that you've spied in the fridge, housed in a cardboard box made to look like a barrel. After one sip of this toe-curling 11 per cent Lucozade-hued nectar, you stop to notice all the locals – who keep referring to you as 'city boy' even though you're from Nuneaton – are drinking Heineken, before losing your vision entirely.

3: Mulled wine

A tipple you thankfully don't see very much outside of the festive season. Perhaps for harmony's sake it's for the best to keep it contained within one month, as letting someone loose on your kitchen to make mulled wine can easily spoil Christmas. They take your best bottle of Châteauneuf-du-Pape and boil it up with Satsuma peel and bits of stick, resulting in hot, sour wine and every room of the house smelling like a festive Airwick Plug-in has exploded, with the added bonus that all your best pans are now ruined. Cheers!

4: *Question Time*

Every episode of *QT* is identical to the last, only some of the names change. There's the MP who brings every question back to their gritty constituency in North-East London. There's a well-to-do nervous chap with a blue tie, who blushes and stutters as he gets talked over. There's someone repeatedly saying, 'I think the best course of action ... will be to sit down ... and work out ... the right solution ... to these problems,' in an attempt to hide the fact they haven't understood the question. Then there's either Peter Hitchins or George Galloway, to give the audience someone to boo, and finally an artist or poet who gets the loudest applause by occasionally asking why we can't all just get along. You almost get the feeling they haven't a clue what they're on about.

5: Camping holidays

You wake up, crumpled, either delirious with heat stroke or numb with cold, with a mouth dryer than a toaster's crumb tray. While scraping a moist cloth across your face (which turns alarmingly brown), you attempt to heat water on a camping stove which, like your tent, is on the brink of collapse. While the water begins to bubble (approximately four hours later) you have enough time for the indignity of visiting the

nearest convenience, carrying lavatory paper upon your person so fellow campers know exactly what you're up to. What's more, your mobile stopped working a few days ago, your blow-up bed has all the rigidity of a soufflé in a disco and the man pitched next you has brought his ukulele. Was that a spot of rain I just felt?

6: Pub roasts

The closest thing to school dinners an adult can eat. Only forkfuls in to your leathery beef, pork as dry as a mouse mat or 'half' a chicken covered in skin with the taste and texture of salty clingfilm, and you're looking enviously at the fish and chips belonging to the one man who was brave enough to go out on a limb and say, 'No! I don't want one to pay £14.20 for one cold slice of meat and half a plate of disintegrating cauliflower, so I'm going to order something nice.' Bravo, sir.

7: Bloody Marys

Regardless of how many Brits claim to benefit from the pick-me-up corpse revival of a Bloody Mary after a night on the sauce, there remains a reason tomato juice is the fullest jug at the hotel breakfast buffet. And if you're going to put Worcestershire sauce and Tabasco in your drink, why stop there? Why not add a dash of HP, or some salad cream? Or simply boil up some pasta and pour it on that? But, having said that, it does provide the one and only acceptable way to drink vodka of a morning, so as you were.

8: Eating out

After receiving an awful meal for which you have just expressed eternal gratification, you're presented with a machine which suggests that if you'd like to leave a gratuity, you should press the yellow button. Despite the terrible service, you still wish to tip, of course, but in cash. Thus follows the sudden fear that a klaxon will go off, with a sign flashing 'tight sod' above your head, as soon as you press the 'no thanks' green button. In a panic you press red, causing receipt paper to spool all over the floor while the waiter stares at you incredulously. At least you've been able to reach the toilets easily, but only because the table the restaurant found you is very nearly in it.

9: Bank holiday DIY

Bank holiday Monday means that by law you shall put on an old shirt, dust off the toolbox and set about ruining your house. After twelve hours of hammering screws into walls and drilling through 5,000V cables, all you've achieved is making your neighbour weep and turning your thumbnails black. Just like last time. You won't be back into work on Tuesday either, as you have to wait for a professional to visit in order to fix everything, while you hide in the kitchen making tea and blaming your spouse for all the mess.

10: Sunday papers

'Money section? No, thank you; Travel? Nope, can't afford it; Appointments? No, I'm not nearly qualified enough for those jobs; Restaurants? Another three-star review? Boring; Business ... yawn; Sport ... throw it away, I don't want to relive my team's thrashing; News? Nah, it's all depressing anyway ... '

When you finish dissecting the huge bundle of expensive paper into the recycling bin, you realise that the only section you like is missing this week. And your favourite columnist is away, replaced by some chap called Rod with a perm, who's upset about having to use three different types of bin.

16. FOOD AND DRINK DILEMMAS

Plucking up the confidence to admit you're completely indifferent towards Marmite.

Never failing to underestimate the power of horseradish.

Being prepared to argue to the death, at any given moment, over the correct method of making tea.

Actually favouring the Toffee Penny, but feeling you must pretend otherwise.

Being too polite to take the last roast potato, and so allowing it to be thrown away.

Having condiments in your fridge that you can't bring yourself to discard, despite them first being opened when Thatcher was in power.

The impossibility of eating a Jaffa Cake without someone bringing up *that* debate.

Panicking in a sandwich shop and allowing a distressingly odd combination of fillings to happen.

Misjudging the biting point on the squeezy HP and unleashing a sauce tsunami towards your bacon sandwich.

Discovering a wet spoon has
recently entered the sugar,
and vowing not to have guests
round again for a while.

Feeling very uncomfortable lying to the self-checkout about how many of your own bags you just used.

Tea bags in the sink.

Feeling mortified if unable to provide a particular condiment upon request.

The shock of tasting Earl Grey when you expected otherwise.

Saying, 'Oh, I don't remember, just give me a fiver,' despite being in dire straits and knowing full well it came to £6.40 each.

Tying your hands behind your back to stave off the temptation to pour the kettle when only half boiled.

Feeling very nervous about the appropriate level of meat preparation to request from a butcher.

Purchasing a cheese the size of a
tractor wheel rather than say, 'Just a
tiny bit smaller . . . ' for a third time.

Discovering your favourite cereal in a foreign supermarket with a slightly different name and finding it a bit too humorous.

Suspecting that by the time you're 90 you'll have convinced yourself that Curly Wurlys used to be the length of small car.

Missing your tea's optimum drinking temperature by seconds.

Spending an entire meal debating whether to tell someone they have food on their face.

The distress of purchasing a job
lot of biscuits, only to discover
they're too large for your mug.

Feeling an overwhelming desire
for cake as soon as the clock
strikes half-past four.

17. NICE WEATHER WE'RE HAVING

Being able to summon rain simply by washing your car and hanging out your laundry.

Wondering what will come first: Talking dogs or a winter with the optimum amount of grit.

Deciding which loyalty card to sacrifice to de-ice the windscreen.

Secretly hoping it stays cold so there's always something to talk about.

Getting soaked when using your own umbrella to cover a friend's head.

Telling someone they've caught the sun,
to indicate they're burnt to an absolute
crisp.

Feeling quite pleased not to have
lost more than one eye to the
slew of short people wielding
umbrellas.

Having a sky that thinks it
fun to mimic the colour of the
pavement.

Trying to pretend you enjoyed being
hit by a snowball, while hoping nobody
notices you're trembling quite violently.

Vowing never to go camping ever again, approximately 402 times per year.

Being unable to recall
the last time you
ended a conversation
without muttering,
'Roll on summer,
that's what I say.'

Missing winter whenever the faint sound of buzzing causes you to hurl yourself into the nearest cupboard.

Walking into wind so severe your eyebrows are blown from your face.

'Did you see the frost this morning?' Translation: 'I was up a lot earlier than you today and I'd like you to know about it.'

Noticing a small patch of blue sky and immediately purchasing 24 cases of Pimm's.

Referring to eating oven-cooked meat while standing in your kitchen as an 'indoor barbecue'.

Being powerless to the urge to take photographs of heavy rain.

Wearing gloves for so long you forget your actual hands aren't made of red wool.

Worrying you might have just triggered a monsoon by purchasing barbecue food.

Slipping on black ice and worrying that you've just crushed the new packet of biscuits in your bag, as well as being slightly concerned that you may have shattered your hip.

Switching on the television to see someone canoeing down their street at least three times a year.

18. REPRESSING ONE'S RAGE

Finding your favourite part of
the Sunday papers is missing and
taking it as a sign that the day
will not go well.

Gearing yourself up for a rant then receiving very good customer service before you can unleash it, making you even more irritated.

The exhausting exasperation resulting from people who try to enter the lift before you've exited.

Attempting to deal with a queue-jumper by staring fiercely at the back of their head.

Becoming so furious that you beg someone for their pardon.

Someone pressing the button at a pelican crossing when you've clearly just pressed it.

Tutting at someone . . . and they hear you.

Thanking people under your breath as punishment for them not thanking you.

Becoming so livid with the poor service you've received that you go straight home to consider writing a letter.

Accidentally saying 'you're welcome' too loudly when someone hasn't thanked you, and smiling politely when they look straight at you.

Never failing to feel
flabbergasted by the total lack
of queuing protocol at bus
stops.

Trying to keep your composure on realising the milk has gone off at the precise moment it's entering your cup.

The palpable mass relief when an accidental queue-jumper suddenly realises their mistake and retreats.

Telling someone to help themselves, then feeling your chest tighten when they take more than you think they should.

Considering saying, 'Excuse me, do you mind?' when someone repeatedly bumps into you, then remembering how shaky you became when you last attempted it in 1992.

Feeling that actually colliding with anyone in your bumper car would be too beastly, so just gently circling until your time is up.

Losing sleep while you wonder if saying, 'I'm not interested, thank you,' and putting the phone down on the cold caller was maybe a little savage.

Trying to remain calm despite being unable to buy a newspaper without being asked if you'd also like a giant bar of chocolate.

Wondering how many nights in a row *Britain's Got Talent* has to be on before you throw your telly into a lake.

Occasionally folding your arms and activating a tiny head shake to indicate that the Post Office queue is thoroughly out of order and you'll only put up with it for another two hours. Three, maximum.

19. VERY BRITISH UNDERSTATEMENT

. . . A Few Examples from Fact and Fiction

During a suburban dinner party . . .

Death: Silence! I have come for you.
Guests: You mean to . . .
Death: . . . Take you away. That is my purpose. I am Death.
Guests: Well, that's cast rather a gloom over the evening hasn't it?

Monty Python's The Meaning of Life, 1983, Graham Chapman, John Cleese, Terry Gilliam, Eric Idle, Terry Jones, Michael Palin

Blackadder and Darling, shortly before going over the top . . .

Captain Blackadder: How are you feeling, Darling?
Captain Darling: . . . not all that good, Blackadder. Rather hoped I'd get through the whole show. Go back to work at Pratt and Sons, keep wicket for the Croydon Gentlemen, marry Doris . . . Made a note in my diary on the way here. Simply says: 'Bugger.'

'Goodbyeee', *Blackadder Goes Forth*, 1989,
Richard Curtis, Ben Elton

'According to urban legend, during the yuletide of 1948 a Washington DC radio station asked ambassadors from a number of countries in the capital their preferred Christmas gift, and the replies were recorded for a special holiday broadcast.

'The expected answers were intoned: "Peace throughout the world," from the French ambassador; "Freedom for all people enslaved by Imperialism," from the Russian; and then a call went through to Sir Oliver Franks, the representative of Her Majesty's Government. "Well, it's very kind of you to ask," he replied. "I'd quite like a box of crystallised fruit." '

'Peace on earth and a box of fruit', Sandi Toksvig, *Telegraph*, 23 December 2007

'It is not all pleasure, this exploration.'

David Livingstone, shortly before succumbing to malaria and dysentery, 1873

On selling an extremely rare watch at Sotheby's . . .

Del Boy: What was the final score? What exactly did it go for?
Rodney: £6.2 million, so that's . . . just over £3 million each.
Del Boy: Well, we've had worse days.

'Time on Our Hands', *Only Fools and Horses*, 1996, John Sullivan

'The adjective "cross" as a description of his Jove-like wrath that consumed his whole being jarred upon Derek profoundly. It was as though Prometheus, with the vultures tearing his liver, had been asked if he were piqued.'

The Little Warrior, P.G. Wodehouse, 1929

On discovering a guest, to whom Basil had earlier delivered breakfast in bed, has actually been dead since the previous night . . .

Dr Price: You mean to tell me you didn't realise this man was dead?
Basil: Well, people don't talk that much in the morning. Look, I'm just delivering a tray, right. If the guest isn't singing 'Oh, What a Beautiful Morning!', I don't immediately think 'Oh, there's another snuffed it in the night.'

'The Kipper and the Corpse', *Fawlty Towers*, 1979, John Cleese, Connie Booth

'It was rather a serious evening, you know.'

Sir Cosmo Duff-Gordon, on surviving the sinking of the
Titanic, 1912

**Upon being told the guns the Zulu are firing were
taken from British soldiers . . .**

Lieutenant Gonville Bromhead: Well, that's a bitter
pill, our own damn rifles.

Zulu, 1964, John Prebble, Cy Enfield

After Clark Griswold knocks a British chap off his bike . . .

Clark: I think you've got a bad cut there, we better get you to the hospital.
British chap: It's just a flesh wound honestly, nothing to write home about, nothing to bother matron. Honestly, it's just a leg, I've got another one.

National Lampoon's Vacation, 1983, John Hughes

'My grandfather, Lieutenant Frederick Gurney Salter, served with 2nd Battalion The Rifle Brigade, who landed in northern France in late 1914. He became eligible for the Silver War Badge, awarded to those invalided out, in 1915. His injured right leg became gangrenous, while he insisted that others' injuries should be tended to before his, and he thereby lost the leg. My father in later life also neglected an injury to his right foot which subsequently became gangrenous and resulted in the loss of *his* right leg. Needless to say I am not at all British now when it comes to my own foot and leg injuries.'

Colin Salter (colinsalter.co.uk), writer, via @soverybritish

'A bit sticky, things are a bit sticky down there.'

British Brigadier Thomas Brodie facing 10,000 Chinese soldiers with 650 men. South Korea, 1951

'We are in a very tight corner.'

Captain Robert Falcon Scott, writing to his wife, on running out of fuel and food, South Pole, 1912

'Last week I saw a woman flayed, and you will hardly believe how much it altered her person for the worse.'

A Tale of a Tub, Jonathan Swift, 1704

'Ladies and gentlemen, this is your captain speaking. We have a small problem. All four engines have stopped. We are doing our damnedest to get them going again. I trust you are not in too much distress.'

Captain Eric Moody, British Airways Flight 9, 1982

Soon after escaping some rather persistent sexual advances from Withnail's very large and very randy Uncle Monty . . .

Marwood: Withnail, you bastard, wake up. Wake up, you bastard or I burn this bastard bed down!
Withnail: (*Stirring*) I deny all accusations. What do you want?
Marwood: I have just narrowly avoided having a buggering. And I've come in here with the express intention of wishing one on you. Having said that, I now intend to leave for London.

Withnail & I, 1987, Bruce Robinson

'I am just going outside and may be some time.'

Captain Lawrence Oates, before walking into an Antarctic blizzard to face a certain demise, 1912

Following William's discovery, during an unexpected encounter at The Ritz, that Anna has a Hollywood boyfriend . . .

Max: Let's face facts, this was always a no-win situation. Anna's a goddess; you know what happens to mortals who get involved with gods.
William: Buggered, is it?
Max: Every time.

Notting Hill, 1999, Richard Curtis

'I did a play with Paul Eddington and he had a much-treasured thing, from a hotel room in Bristol during the war, which was just a card with a little bit of cord. It said "Please hang outside your room if you wish to be awoken during an air raid." Splendidly phlegmatic.'

Stephen Fry, 'Inequality and Injustice', *QI*, 2011

After trying to explain to Arthur Dent that he (Ford) is not actually from Guildford, but from a planet in the vicinity of Betelgeuse . . .

'Ford gave up. It really wasn't worth bothering at the moment, what with the world being about to end. He just said:
    "Drink up."
    He added, perfectly factually:
    "The world's about to end."
    Arthur gave the rest of the pub another wan smile. The rest of the pub frowned at him. A man waved at him to stop smiling at them and mind his own business.

"This must be Thursday," said Arthur musing to himself, sinking low over his beer, "I never could get the hang of Thursdays.'"

The Hitchhiker's Guide to the Galaxy, Douglas Adams, 1978

'If you are going through hell, keep going.'

Winston Churchill

20. APOLOGISING . . .

. . . to furniture, when you bump into it.

. . . to a stranger for not smoking, and then giving directions towards someone who possibly has a lighter.

. . . to a mystery caller because you think they may have dialled the wrong number.

. . . as a way of catching someone's attention.

. . . when entering a lift.

. . . for asking a taxi driver if he minds stopping at a cash point, as if there's a chance he'd prefer it if you didn't pay.

. . . to your boss for asking to take the time off you didn't take last year.

. . . for attempting to haggle, before paying full price, and sometimes more.

. . . profusely immediately after asking anyone for the time, and then once again after you've thanked them for giving you the time.

. . . to tourists for the
inclement weather.

. . . for being late, despite actually being on time and the person you're meeting being early.

. . . for informing someone they've dropped their purse.

. . . to the person who has waited for you to leave the lavatory, despite only spending 20 fruitless seconds in there because you couldn't take the pressure.

. . . for 'only' having a ten-pound note when paying for a £9 item.

. . . because you think someone
may be standing on your foot.

. . . for finishing your meal first/last.

**. . . for asking a fellow
commuter if you may borrow
their bag's seat for a short
while.**

. . . to the paramedics for
troubling them over something as
silly as a stroke.

. . . for opening a door for someone
which turns out to be much heavier than
expected, providing a gap that is far
from ideal.

. . . to the jolly chap who just
rammed a shopping trolley into
your leg.

. . . for getting in the way of the person cycling on the pavement.

. . . for getting in the taxi that pulled up for you, after the person behind you just tried to steal it.

. . . for being tired.

. . . for having the audacity to put an extra item on the counter after you've already been told the price of your other goods.

. . . to your boss for being late, despite the fact that you both arrived at exactly the same time.

. . . for reaching to get your bag from the luggage rack, despite being on an empty train.

. . . to the barman because the ale you wanted has run out.

. . . for apologising so much.

. . . for no reason whatsoever.

21. LANGUAGE BARRIERS

Telling someone you're speaking to them 'with all due respect' to indicate you disagree with their point of view entirely.

Saying something was 'quite good' to indicate how truly terrible it was.

Saying you'll 'bear something in mind', thus indicating your plan to forget all about it almost immediately.

Wondering whether to ask 'how are you doing?' or 'how's it going?', then getting flustered and asking, 'how's it doing?'

Saying that somebody's comment is certainly 'food for thought', as an indication that your last thought ever on the matter has just occurred.

Using 'honestly, it's fine' to warn of your imminent meltdown.

Sounding sarcastic no matter how many ways you try saying 'that sounds great'.

Saying, 'Correct me if I'm wrong,' to indicate that you know you're right and do not wish to be contradicted.

'No no, after you, you were next . . . ' Translation: you were very much not next, you abrasive sod.

Saying, 'Look, I'm not going to argue with you about this any longer,' to subtly indicate you've realised you're wrong.

Feeling disappointed when encouraged to 'do the math'.

Saying, 'It's a bit chilly,' to indicate you've lost the feeling in your feet and your toes have turned black.

Declaring yourself 'quite chuffed', to indicate you're the most pleased you've ever been

Saying, 'Let's come back to that,' meaning, 'Please don't speak again in this meeting.'

Trying not to be the person who can't wait to call something 'very Orwellian' in conversation.

Saying, 'Thanks very much, cheers, ta,' as a way of thanking someone once.

Being forced to use emoticons in text messages to alert people that you're definitely *not* being sarcastic.

Proclaiming the most terrible of situations to be not in any way comparable to cricket.

Saying, 'Yes, we should definitely do that sometime,' to indicate you will never be meeting up for dinner. Ever.

Saying, 'I shouldn't
really, but go on then,
if you're having one?'
instead of the more
economical 'yes'.

Informing someone that your pet might give them 'a bit of a nip', to warn it will take their arm clean off at any given opportunity.

Saying, 'Yeah, go on then, why not?' to indicate you fully intend to have another drink, if not four.

Never wanting to use an exclamation mark yet worrying you'll come across as miserable without one.

Saying, 'I'll take your word for it.' Meaning: 'You don't know what you're talking about.'

Saying 'bugger' to warn
others that you've just stood
in a bear trap.

22. NO SEX PLEASE ...

Deciding to spice things up a bit, so switching from pitch-darkness to leaving the hallway light on.

Noticing someone smiling at you and immediately assuming there's something terribly wrong with your face.

Not asking someone you find attractive if they fancy doing something at the weekend, in case they have plans.

Wondering if you've left it too late to take your socks off, and then pausing to ask.

Bumping into someone you've been on a few dates with while carrying your recently purchased multipack of loo roll, thus revealing the terrible secret that you use the toilet.

Accidentally touching someone's hand on your commute and immediately worrying they think you're a pervert.

Wondering if you should put the kettle on beforehand, so it'll be about boiled by the time you're done and dusted.

Receiving an email from a colleague that ends with an 'x', resulting in you having to sit outside and get some fresh air for a bit.

Catching someone's eye on the train, quickly looking away and then immediately catching their eye in the window reflection. Wondering if you should propose.

Despite the fact that you are now 43, turning bright red when you're watching television with your parents and the actors so much as hug.

Replying, 'No I don't,' when someone says you look good.

Lowering the passion a hefty notch
every time you say, 'Oops, hang on.'

Wondering how people on telly
manage to copulate outdoors,
when you know if you tried it
you'd end up scaring a cow and
rolling in a thistle.

**Seriously considering
engaging in conversation
with that attractive fellow
commuter. For eight years.**

Suspecting the moment ended at the point when you rolled over and burst the hot-water bottle.

Knowing you'll be going home alone the minute you realise you've started throwing in a random hand-clap while 'dancing'.

Having a cupboard containing 200 packets of ibuprofen, because you keep getting embarrassed in Boots.

Working up such a sweat that you consider buying a less insulated thermal vest.

Wondering whether you should expand your chat-up line armoury beyond 'how do you do?' and 'I think you're nice'.

23. FUTURE VERY BRITISH PROBLEMS

Making Life Awkward for Ourselves, One Rainy Day at a Time (Until Records Cease)

2014

The rise of augmented-reality glasses results in countless Brits with thousand-yard stares having to say 'sorry, I wasn't looking at you' up to fifty times a day.

2018

All online food shopping is now a virtual reality supermarket experience, complete with virtual trolleys ramming into your leg. Click 'sorry' within two seconds of this happening and you'll receive double loyalty points.

2020

The bowler hat comes back into fashion.

2025

Brits are used to being forced to use emoticons to show they're not being sarcastic, but by 2025 people speak *entirely* in emoticons, one of which will mean 'no sarcasm intended', which will often be used sarcastically.

2027

Jamie Oliver's new book *30 Second Meals* sells one billion copies in its first week. People complain the meals take them up to a whole minute to create.

2029

A once-a-year injection is developed which freezes hairstyles at optimum length, meaning Brits never have to pretend to like their new haircut ever again.

2030

A pint of beer now costs £20. People reminisce about how once they only had to hand over a fiver.

2032

Holographic TV will be commonplace in all homes, meaning you'll be able to see British tennis players losing in five-set semi-final thrillers as if Wimbledon is in your living room, complete with a robotically enhanced Cliff Richard and four holographic strawberries for £16.

2034

Someone finally picks Acid Jazz as their category in the final round of *Pointless*.

2035

Supersonic bullet trains will take just 15 minutes to get passengers from London to Edinburgh, meaning Brits will stand to queue, ready to exit the train, after only five minutes of sitting down.

2038

3D Printers are now capable of printing cups of tea. After numerous instances of people dipping the coffee cartridge into the sugar cartridge, and after users twig it essentially does the same job as vending machine but takes ten hours longer, popularity wanes.

2040

Sir David Beckham becomes king.

2042

All our food comes in pill form, meaning no more having to wait for your colleagues to leave the office before eating your lunch at speed, lest they witness you anxiously dripping mayonnaise onto your mouse mat.

2045

The wettest year since records began.

2046

Hosepipes banned permanently.

2047

Poor viewing figures for *The Only Way is Nantwich* persuade producers that the format is in need of a refresh.

2048

A 99 ice cream now costs £2,000.

2050

Space elevators made from carbon nanotubes twenty times stronger than steel are able to carry 30 passengers to the stars at 125mph. Although speedy, the journey will still take seven days – a staggering amount of time to avoid eye contact, not to mention the unspoken issue of potentially life-threatening in-lift flatulence.

2055

Pubs ban alcohol inside, forcing people to sup beverages in designated outside drinking areas.

2056

All jobs in the UK now have to be 'won' by successfully completing nine weeks of tasks set by the 110-year-old Emperor Alan Sugar.

2057

Not everyone agrees with Harry Potter featuring on the new £1,000 note, and there's even more debate about Russell Brand for the £500. Everyone seems quite pleased with Alan Partridge on the £200, however.

2058

Mr Blobby comes out of retirement to win Eurovision for the UK. He goes on to a sell-out arena tour, supported by recently reunited boy band, One Direction.

2060

Britain's ageing population means one in four people are over the age of 65, making the arrival of robot cleaners all the more welcome. Brits still feel the need to tidy up the house a bit before activating them, though.

2062

Bruce Forsyth retires.

2066

England reach the World Cup finals against Germany, but lose after a last-minute goal is disallowed by the robotic goalposts.

2067

Every single inanimate object in Britain now features a Keep Calm and Carry On logo.

2070

Cars are completely driver-free, with the one remaining British model programmed to flash every indicator, hazard and headlamp three times when another car lets it by, though this hasn't happened for at least twenty years.

2072

The Rolling Stones release a statement saying their next album will be their last, as Keith Richards has decided he wants to concentrate on solo projects.

2077

The British start moving to Mars, twenty one years after the first Earthlings landed on the Red Planet. After the eight-month journey, seven months of which were spent quietly seething about the people who reclined their seats, the Brits emerge from the hold to proclaim the weather 'a bit muggy', before scanning for the nearest greasy spoon.

2081

The last ever episode of *EastEnders* sees Dirty Den return for the eighteenth time. Everybody dies.

2082

The Rolling Stones reform for a series of one-off shows.

2090

It is now 77 years since a Brit last won Wimbledon. As the latest British number 1 is about to hit his first serve of the tournament, the crowd chuckle as someone shouts 'Come on, Tim!' – though nobody can remember what this actually means – as Sir Cliff Richard looks on.

2099

An asteroid plummets towards Earth. Seconds before impact, the sound of every Brit (81 million of them living in the UK by this point in time) muttering the word 'bugger' causes a sonic vibration of such force that the giant rock shatters to dust. Millions of kettles are then boiled in celebration.

2111

Tea runs out. Britain crumbles, and Paul McCartney's brain in a jar is brought out to sing 'Hey Jude' as the nation is washed out to sea.

24. PUBLIC SPEAKING

The overwhelming dread which accompanies the sentence: 'Before we start, let's just go round the table and say a bit about ourselves.'

Losing faith in your delivery halfway through telling a joke, so opting to just explain what the punch line was going to be and why.

Apologising while pretending there's a sentence in your notes that you can't quite make out, rather than tell the planned joke that you can read perfectly clearly.

The fear of being encouraged to 'do that impression you do'.

Making a phone call just as your whole office decides to fall silent, causing you to forget how to speak.

The terror of hearing that later you'll be required to present your ideas to the room.

Staying in the same job forever to avoid any possible leaving speech scenario.

Willing yourself invisible on hearing the question, 'Do we have a volunteer?'

Immediately insulting anyone who hints you may be one of their closest friends, to keep any 'Best Man' ideas at bay.

The collective despair when someone raises their hand after the room is asked, 'So, any questions?'

Being more willing to go for a paddle in water known to attract crocodiles than sit in the front row of a stand-up comedy performance.

Asking an interviewer if you could just take a minute to think of your answer to their question because you've read somewhere that this looks impressive, and spending that minute thinking of nothing whatsoever.

Suspecting you're about to be asked to say a few words, so knocking yourself unconscious with the nearest brick.

The pure horror of
mentioning a song
and being asked,
'How does it go?'

Foolishly having a go at an accent during a joke and ending up sounding Welsh, unless it's Welsh you were attempting, in which case you sound Indian.

Considering Colin Firth's pre-therapy public speaking in *The King's Speech* as something to aim for.

Thinking nobody notices every time you only mime the first three lines of 'Happy Birthday To You'.

Accidentally going to an interactive theatre production.

Beginning the PowerPoint presentation you spent three weeks on with, 'This is really rough, so . . . ' and then skipping through nearly every slide.

Being asked what your biggest achievement is in a job interview. A question no British person should ever have to face.

The terror of struggling through a conversation where you've just lied about having seen, read or even heard of the subject at hand.

25. AVIATION AGGRAVATION

Feeling utter disbelief when someone manages to bring a suitcase-sized item of hand luggage on to the aircraft.

Protecting your area at baggage recall as if the lives of your family depend on it.

Wishing your phone had an Aeroplane Mode rather than an Airplane Mode.

Affecting either
a Jamie Oliver or
Hugh Grant accent
when abroad,
depending on blood-
alcohol levels.

Watching aghast as someone reclines their seat.

Rushing to be the first in the queue at the departure gate, despite booking a specific seat five months previously.

Turning a film off because you suspect a sex scene may be about to happen and you don't want your fellow passengers to think you're a deviant who enjoys eating a sausage and mash ready-meal while watching erotica.

Never under any circumstance pressing the call button on a plane, in case you disturb the cabin crew.

Forgetting to remove your book before stowing away your bag and taking the window seat, meaning you won't see it again for nine hours.

Finding yourself sitting next to someone who asks you if England is in London.

Feeling the need to stand up as soon as the seatbelt sign has deactivated, despite having to bend your neck at a violent angle and knowing it'll be at least quarter of an hour before the doors open.

Wondering if you should
walk up and down the cabin
to stretch your legs, but being
paralysed by stage fright.

Being unable to let a wonky bag
go by on the carousel without
straightening it up and sending it
on its way.

The nervy, unnatural feeling of having
boiling liquid poured into a cup that's
balanced on a tiny tray being held above
your face, 30,000 feet above ground.

Allowing your bladder to explode rather than wake a fellow plane passenger.

The silent fury of getting caught behind someone who has decided to stand on the travelator.

Only doing what your neighbouring passengers do with the mini hot towel. If they don't go face, you don't go face.

Finding you've not been provided with a knife, so experiencing – not for the first time – how hard it is to butter a bread roll with a spoon.

Leaving a light on before abandoning your house for two weeks, in the hope any burglars will be convinced you spend the entirety of your evenings in the hallway.

The overwhelming urge to drink
every last bit of booze in your
house the night before a flight.

**Throwing in the towel on
a decade of vegetarianism
because they've given you a
meat meal and you don't want
to be awkward.**

Adding four hours onto your
return journey to account for
the time you'll spend hunting
throughout the small hours for a
milk-selling newsagent.

Feeling horrified to see that the man in Bermuda shorts and flip-flops has been upgraded, when you're wearing a white linen jacket and your best straw hat and remain in economy.

26. THE MINEFIELD OF MANNERS

Going through a door because it's being held for you, regardless of your intended destination.

Getting stuck in a 'fine thanks, how are you?' loop.

Discovering it's a push door as you open it for someone, making them squeeze by in a flurry of apologies.

Saying you don't mind when offered a choice, then praying you're left with the option you want.

Being told to enjoy your meal, flight, stay or birthday and replying, 'Thanks, you too!'

Hoping your friend finishes their story
so you don't have to miss your bus stop.

**Feeling weird asking
someone to take their shoes
off, so just letting them ruin
your carpet.**

Feeling guilty about being called
through to your GP when you were the
last to arrive in the waiting room.

Looking away so violently as
someone nearby enters their pin
that you dislocate your neck.

Stoically accepting your
role as a doorman to an
unexpectedly long queue of
people.

Being resigned to
living your entire
life without ever
experiencing the taste
of the last biscuit.

The uncomfortable moment when someone realises you've been allowing them to get your name wrong for quite some time.

Hoping somebody else pushed the stop button on the bus, so as not to be the one who inconveniences the driver.

Offering your seat to an elderly person who on closer inspection turns out to be younger than first thought, so you both stand.

Letting someone go ahead of you in a revolving door and then feeling you have to surreptitiously push them round from behind.

Not wanting to tell someone they've misheard you, so simply soldiering into a completely different topic of conversation.

Holding the door for someone with the tip of your outstretched foot, to indicated you've really no time to dilly-dally.

Agreeing with someone who says the room is too hot and actually taking off a layer, despite feeling that the temperature is perfectly reasonable.

Not wanting to be rude and ring the bell at a hotel reception, standing there for half a day waiting for someone to notice you, then being told off for not ringing the bell. Apologising.

Opening a door for someone who is miles away, causing them to develop a hernia sprinting to earn your chivalry.

Saying of course you remember the childhood TV show your friend has just spent ten minutes describing, despite not having a clue what he's talking about.

Running out of ways to say thank you when a succession of doors are held for you, having already deployed 'cheers', 'ta' and 'nice one'.

Inviting someone to 'drop by anytime' . . . and then they do.

Getting locked into an 'after you, I insist' battle of wills with a stranger.

27. THE VERY BRITISH GLOSSARY

The Most Commons Words and Phrases Used by the British

Bee's knees (The)

Something rather agreeable, such as a particularly nice marmalade or a brand new hat.

Blimey

A reaction upon hearing some rather surprising information, e.g.: 'Blimey, it's stopped raining ...'

Bloody

Absolute. E.g. The 'bloody doors' were to be blown off, and nothing more.

Bob's your uncle

'And there you have it.' Can occasionally mean a man called Robert is one of your parent's brothers, but this is rare.

Bugger

Expression of dismay after experiencing anything from a minor upset (slicing your foot off with the lawnmower) to unthinkable tragedy (missing your tea's optimum drinking temperature).

Cheeky

Sly, secretive, mischievous. E.g. 'a cheeky pint'.

Cheers

Thanks, goodbye or good wishes before drinking. Cheers can often be meant sarcastically, though it is very hard to tell when this is happening.

Cheesed off

Jolly annoyed. Opposite of 'chuffed'.

Chuffed

Happiness/pride ranging anywhere from quite pleased to positively euphoric.

Codswallop

Absolute nonsense. Often shouted by Brits while listening to *Question Time*.

Cricket (It's just not)

A situation, occurrence or remark that is completely unacceptable and undesirable in every way.

Dilly-dally

To waste time or dawdle, often in indecision.

Dog's bollocks

Actually a good thing. Vulgar version of 'bee's knees'; similar in meaning, but more so.

Fancy (To)

To find someone attractive.

Fancy the pants off (To)

To find someone very attractive indeed.

Fine

E.g. 'It's fine'. Meaning: It's not fine. If a Brit describes something as 'fine' it means he/she is perilously close to becoming cheesed off and saying 'bugger'.

Flabbergasted

Shocked or greatly surprised.

Flummoxed

Baffled nearly to the point of stroking your chin and glowering in concentration.

Gap year

A 12-month holiday taken by a British students, between leaving school and starting further education, in order to collect colourful beaded jewellery from hot countries.

Glower

To stare silently in a sullen or angry manner, usually at a queue-jumper or a Quiet Coach chatterbox in the hope they'll disintegrate.

Gobsmacked

Taken aback. A mixture of flabbergasted and flummoxed. Can result in expressions of 'blimey'.

Gutted

Used to convey utter dismay at a terrible situation, such as your favourite sports team suffering a loss, or the death of a loved one.

Knackered

Extreme weariness, usually the first word said by most British office workers on a Monday morning.

Mate

Name for a friend, enemy, complete stranger or someone whose name you have repeatedly failed to grasp.

Not bad

Good. Better than expected.

Not bad at all

Absolutely fantastic. Much better than expected.

Not my cup of tea

'I do not like this person/place/thing in any way whatsoever.'

Oops-a-daisy

Said in order to acknowledge a mistake or upon dropping something/tripping over.

Plastered

Severely intoxicated by alcohol, to the point of purchasing a Styrofoam tray of chips and hurling it toward the pavement.

Pop round

E.g. 'I'll pop round later'. To visit someone's house for a short period of time. Brits will respond to someone saying this in a positive and encouraging manner, while strongly considering moving house in case it does actually happen.

Quite good

Absolutely terrible. Much worse than expected.

Skew-whiff

Crooked. E.g. 'What's wrong with your hair/face/shirt? It's all skew-whiff.'

Skint

To be lacking in money. Usually claimed dishonestly as part of an effort to avoid getting plastered following eight cheeky pints.

Shambles

A chaotic mess. E.g. 'England's defence has been an absolute shambles during this tournament/since 1974'.

Shirty

Bad tempered, aggressive.

Sorry

Uttered more than any other word in a Brit's vocabulary, as an expression of apology, as a greeting or simply for no reason whatsoever.

Spiffing

Jolly good.

Stag Night

Traditional punishment for getting married; typically involves alcohol, lampposts, amnesia and/or permanent regret.

Roundabout

Circular road junction. Politeness often causes British drivers to be stuck at small versions of these, sometimes for years at a time.

Ta

Thank you. Usually said on receiving a drink in a pub to show the barman you're on his level.

Tickety-boo

Used to describe a situation that is going spiffingly.

Trolley (Off your)

To exhibit signs of madness. Also commonly used:
Bonkers; Barking.

Trollied

See 'Plastered'.

Trousered

See 'Plastered'.

Zonked

Tired. See 'Knackered'.

ACKNOWLEDGEMENTS

Thanks to all the VBP sufferers who follow @soverybritish; to my very good friend Adam Bunker for 'Tweet Testing' and suggesting more than a few entries for this book; cheers to Matt for saying I should start a Twitter feed and James for inspiring the theme. Huge thanks and very un-British high-fives to my awesome agent Juliet Mushens and my fantastic editor Hannah Boursnell and all the team at Little, Brown/Sphere. Huge cheers to Andrew Wightman for bringing *Very British Problems* to life with so many wonderful, hilarious illustrations. Thanks to Rhiain, and my new Welsh family, for putting up with an awkward Englishman. And my eternal gratitude to my immediate family, Lisa, Mark, Pete, Jane, Finlay, Freya, Emily and James, for all the inspiration, retweets and fun. And lastly but mostly, thank you to my Mum and Dad, for your constant support, encouragement and pints of Pimm's.

Sorry to bother you again . . .

If you would rate this book as either 'not bad' or 'not bad at all' (steady on), may we suggest that you follow @soverybritish on Twitter for more Very British mishaps and misunderstandings?

And if it's not too much trouble, you might also consider joining in by using the hashtag #verybritishproblems.

There's also a plethora of Very British Problems over at Facebook, should you feel inclined to 'like' the page at www.facebook.com/soverybritish

Thanks awfully.